# EMPOWERING AFFIRMATIONS FOR BLACK WOMEN

1000 DAILY POSITIVE AND INSPIRATIONAL
AFFIRMATIONS FOR BIPOC WOMEN TO FOSTER
HAPPINESS, HEALTH, SUCCESS, ENHANCE
CONFIDENCE, AND SELF-LOVE

SERENITY BEAUMONT

# CONTENTS

# INTRODUCTION

As you begin this journey of affirmations, envision yourself in a space of openness and receptivity. These affirmations are crafted to be more than words; they are a celebration of your identity as a black woman, designed to influence and uplift your spirit. Allow these positive statements to affect your mindset, one that promotes self-love, confidence, and success to flourish. Approach each affirmation with positive intention, one that builds strength and purpose.

Recognize the power these affirmations hold—they are not only reflections of your individuality but also acknowledgments of the collective strength, resilience, and beauty of black women throughout history. As you absorb these words, visualize the positive impact they can have on your self-worth, relationships, and aspirations.

Embrace a mindset of abundance and possibility. Let these affirmations serve as daily reminders of your potential, and the extraordinary qualities that make you unique. Picture yourself stepping into each day with confidence, fueled by the positivity and self-love that stems from these affir-mations.

In this mindset, you become an inspiration of strength and self-love to those around you. Allow these affirmations to not only transform your thoughts, but also shape your actions, leading you toward a path of success, happiness, and fulfillment. Embrace the journey, celebrate your identity, and let these affirmations empower you to manifest the life you desire.

# EMPOWERING AFFIRMATIONS FOR BLACK WOMEN

I am deserving of love, success, and happiness.

My strength is a source of inspiration to others.

I embrace my unique beauty and radiance.

Success flows effortlessly to me.

I am a powerful creator of my destiny.

Abundance is my birthright, and I claim it now.

~

I am a vessel of positivity and light.

~

Confidence is my second nature.

~

I embody clarity, navigating decisions with a focused and clear mind, a skill honed by the wisdom of my unique journey.

~

I attract peace effortlessly, finding tranquility within myself and fostering an environment of serenity for those around me.

~

I am a resilient creator, transforming challenges into opportunities for growth, drawing strength from the rich tapestry of my heritage.

~

I radiate joy, becoming a beacon of happiness and spreading the light of positivity to uplift the black women in my community.

～

I am a source of innovative ideas, bringing forth creativity that reflects the richness of black culture and experiences.

～

I align my actions with purpose, attracting positive intentions that resonate with the values and aspirations of black women.

～

I safeguard my energy, intentionally surrounding myself with positivity that aligns with the vibrancy of the black community.

～

I am a champion for balance, harmonizing the diverse aspects of my life in a way that reflects the resilience and strength of black women.

～

I express gratitude, recognizing the beauty in both challenges and triumphs within the black woman's journey.

～

I attract success effortlessly, opening my arms to accomplishments that celebrate the brilliance of black women across all fields.

～

I embody courage, facing fears with bravery and resilience, inspired by the legacy of strong black women who paved the way.

～

I motivate myself and others, drawing inspiration from the achievements of black women who reached new heights against all odds.

～

I attract abundance in various forms, reflecting the prosperity that stems from the diverse talents and contributions of black women.

～

I nurture my well-being, honoring the body, mind, and spirit, acknowledging the importance of self-care in the black woman's narrative.

∼

I contribute to positive change, actively working towards a better world that recognizes and celebrates the unique perspectives of black women.

∼

I embody authenticity, embracing my true self without reservation, adding to the diverse tapestry of black women's stories.

∼

I empower myself and others, recognizing the strength and capabilities inherent in the essence of being a black woman.

∼

I attract loving relationships, surrounded by genuine connections that celebrate the richness and diversity within the black community.

∼

I champion self-compassion, extending kindness and understanding to myself, an essential part of the self-love journey for black women.

~

I am a source of wisdom, gaining insights from every experience.

~

I attract growth effortlessly, evolving into the best version of myself, inspired by the continual growth and progress within the black community.

~

I safeguard my dreams, pursuing them with determination and passion, echoing the perseverance of black women who dared to dream.

~

I create serenity, finding peace amid life's uncertainties.

~

I radiate positive vibrations, elevating the energy around me and contributing to the collective vibrancy of the black experience.

~

I am a vessel of inspiration, igniting creativity in myself and others, celebrating the richness and diversity of black artistic expression.

~

I attract opportunities aligned with my purpose, reflecting the boundless possibilities that arise from the unique gifts of black women.

~

I champion self-love, recognizing and celebrating my inherent worthiness, contributing to a narrative of empowerment for black women.

~

I am a source of encouragement, providing unwavering support to others.

~

I guard my boundaries, honoring and protecting my space.

~

I am a creator of joy, infusing laughter and happiness into my days.

~

I celebrate the joyous spirit that defines the essence of being a black woman.

～

I am resilient, no challenge can break me.

～

My journey is a testament to my strength.

～

I attract prosperity in all areas of my life.

～

Love and joy surround me every day.

～

My self-love is the foundation of my well-being.

～

I am open to receiving all the good that life has to offer.

～

Wealth and success manifest easily for me.

～

Every step I take is a step toward greatness.

～

My presence brings positivity to any room.

～

I radiate confidence, self-assuredness, and grace.

～

I celebrate the magic within me.

～

Success and abundance are drawn to me.

～

My mind is a magnet for positive thoughts.

～

I release all self-doubt and embrace my power.

～

I am a beacon of love and kindness.

～

I am deserving of all the good things life has to offer.

~

I am in control of my own happiness.

~

I trust in my ability to achieve my goals.

~

I am a beacon of elegance, carrying myself with grace and sophistication, reflecting the refined strength inherent in black women.

~

I attract prosperity effortlessly, welcoming abundance into my life in ways that align with the resilience and brilliance of black women.

~

I am a curator of cultural richness, embracing and celebrating the diverse heritage that defines the essence of being a black woman.

~

I am a harmonizer of relationships, fostering unity and understanding within the black community, recognizing the strength in our collective bonds.

∾

I embody fearlessness, confronting challenges with a spirit unyielding, echoing the boldness of black women who paved the way for progress.

∾

I am a visionary, casting my gaze towards a future of possibilities that honors and uplifts the aspirations of black women.

∾

I am a maestro of strength, conducting the symphony of my life with resilience, echoing the enduring spirit of black women throughout history.

∾

I am a luminary of self-discovery, continually exploring and embracing the depths of my identity as a black woman.

∾

I radiate elegance, expressing my unique style and flair, contributing to the diverse tapestry of black women's fashion and expression.

∼

I am an alchemist of positivity, transmuting challenges into opportunities for growth and transformation, a testament to the strength of black women.

∼

I am a custodian of heritage, preserving and sharing the stories and traditions that encapsulate the legacy of black women.

∼

I am a navigator of change, embracing the dynamic nature of life and evolving with resilience and adaptability, mirroring the fluid strength of black women.

∼

I am a harmonious force, resonating with the rhythms of life and echoing the melodies of black women's contributions to art, music, and culture.

∼

I am a luminary of love, radiating compassion and kindness, contributing to the nurturing and supportive spirit within the black community.

~

I am a sculptor of destiny, shaping my path with intention and purpose, embodying the agency and determination of black women.

~

I am a conductor of self-expression, leading the orchestra of my life with authenticity, reflecting the diverse and vibrant voices of black women.

~

I am a guardian of joy, cultivating an atmosphere of celebration and happiness, embracing the joyous spirit that defines being a black woman.

~

I am a curator of excellence, consistently striving for greatness in all endeavors.

~

I am a custodian of resilience, preserving and passing down the stories of black women who triumphed over adversity.

~

I am an architect of dreams, building a future filled with possibilities and opportunities that honor the dreams and aspirations of black women.

~

I am a beacon of radiance, shining with an inner light that reflects the brilliance and luminosity of black women.

~

I am a guardian of sisterhood, fostering connections and bonds that amplify the collective strength and support within the black community.

~

I am an orchestrator of empowerment, conducting movements and initiatives that uplift and empower black women globally.

~

I am a curator of wisdom, drawing insights from the rich tapestry of black experiences and history, embodying the wisdom passed down through generations.

~

I am a weaver of dreams, intertwining my aspirations
with the collective dreams of black women.

~

I am a masterpiece, a work of art in progress.
My life is filled with love, joy, and abundance.

~

I am surrounded by supportive and uplifting people.

~

I am a force for positive change in the world.
I attract opportunities that lead to success.

~

My heart is open to giving and receiving love.
I am a resilient and powerful woman.

~

My potential is limitless.

~

I am a source of inspiration for others.

~

I am proud of the person I am becoming.

~

I radiate confidence and grace in every situation.

~

Success and prosperity flow through me.

~

My mind is a magnet for positive energy.

~

I am the architect of my own destiny.

~

Love, success, and happiness are my companions.

~

I embrace my imperfections; they make me unique.

~

My confidence grows stronger every day.

~

Abundance is drawn to me like a magnet.

～

I am worthy of all the good things life has to offer.

～

I trust the journey, even when I do not understand it.

～

My spirit is unbreakable.

～

I attract positivity and repel negativity.

～

I am a magnet for miracles.

～

I release all doubts and embrace my true self.

～

Success is my natural state of being.

～

I am a source of inspiration for others to follow their dreams.

∼

I am surrounded by love and abundance.

∼

I am confident in my abilities to achieve my goals.

∼

My heart is open to giving and receiving love freely.

∼

I am a beacon of light, spreading positivity.

∼

I am deserving of success and all its rewards.

∼

Every challenge I face is an opportunity for growth.

∼

I am a powerful creator of my reality.

∼

I attract positive, like-minded individuals.

~

My self-love empowers me to create a fulfilling life.

~

I am resilient and can overcome any obstacle.

~

I am grateful for the abundance that flows into my life.

~

I am the author of my story, and it is filled with success.

~

I am a masterpiece, a work of art in progress.

~

I attract opportunities that align with my purpose.

~

I am a beacon of love and positivity.

~

My journey is filled with love, joy, and abundance.

~

I am worthy of all the good things life has to offer.

~

I trust in my ability to create the life I desire.

~

I am a force for positive change in the world.

~

Success and prosperity are my natural states of being.

~

My mind is a magnet for positive thoughts.

~

I am a resilient and powerful woman.

~

My potential is limitless.

~

I am proud of the person I am becoming.

∼

I radiate confidence and grace in every situation.

∼

Success and prosperity flow through me.

∼

My heart is open to giving and receiving love.

∼

I am the architect of my own destiny.

∼

Love, success, and happiness are my companions.

∼

I embrace my imperfections; they make me unique.

∼

My confidence grows stronger every day.

∼

Abundance is drawn to me like a magnet.

~

I am worthy of all the good things life has to offer.

~

I trust the journey, even when I do not understand it.

~

My spirit is unbreakable.

~

I attract positivity and repel negativity.

~

I am a magnet for miracles.

~

I release all doubts and embrace my true self.

~

Success is my natural state of being.

~

I am a source of inspiration for others to follow their dreams.

~

I am surrounded by love and abundance.

~

I am confident in my abilities to achieve my goals.

~

My heart is open to giving and receiving love freely.

~

I am a beacon of light, spreading positivity.

~

I am deserving of success and all its rewards.

~

Every challenge I face is an opportunity for growth.

~

I am a powerful creator of my reality.

~

I attract positive, like-minded individuals.

∼

I am worthy of love, success, and happiness.

∼

My beauty radiates from within, reflecting my unique essence.

∼

I attract positive energy, opportunities, and abundance effortlessly.

∼

Success is my natural state; I achieve my goals with grace and determination.

∼

Every step I take leads me toward prosperity and fulfillment.

∼

Confidence is my birthright; I carry myself with self-assuredness and poise.

∼

I am a beacon of light, spreading joy and positivity to those around me.

∾

My mind is a magnet for success; I embrace a mindset of abundance.

∾

I am resilient; challenges are opportunities for growth and strength.

∾

Wealth flows into my life in various forms, and I welcome it with gratitude.

∾

Love surrounds me, and I am open to giving and receiving it fully.

∾

My self-love is the foundation for a fulfilling and joyful life.

∾

I trust in my journey, even when faced with uncertainties.

~

I celebrate my heritage and the richness it adds to my life.

~

Each day, I am becoming the best version of myself.

~

I am a source of inspiration for others to pursue their dreams.

~

I am a powerful creator; my thoughts shape my reality.

~

I release all self-doubt and embrace my true potential.

~

Abundance is drawn to me like a magnet; I am open to receiving it.

~

I am a confident, intelligent, and capable woman. I create my own path.

~

My journey is filled with love, joy, and meaningful connections.

∿

I am deserving of all the good things life has to offer.

∿

I attract positive, like-minded individuals into my life.

∿

My heart is open, and I attract genuine, uplifting relationships.

∿

I am proud of my achievements and embrace the lessons in challenges.

∿

Positivity is my default state; I see the good in every situation.

∿

I am a vessel of creativity, turning my ideas into reality.

∿

My presence exudes confidence, leaving a lasting positive impression.

∾

I am a force for positive change, contributing to the betterment of the world.

∾

I honor and respect myself, setting healthy boundaries in relationships.

∾

I am financially abundant, and money flows easily into my life.

∾

I trust the timing of my life and embrace the unfolding of my journey.

∾

I am a queen, deserving of royal treatment in all aspects of life.

∾

I radiate kindness, compassion, and warmth to those I encounter.

~

Success is not a destination but a continuous journey, and I embrace it.

~

I am in control of my thoughts, choosing positivity and empowerment.

~

I am a magnet for miracles, and I welcome them into my life.

~

I am a valuable and irreplaceable asset to the world.

~

My past does not define me; I create my present and future.

~

I attract opportunities that align with my passions and purpose.

~

My mind is a reservoir of creativity, and I express it freely.

~

I am a beacon of hope, inspiring others to pursue their dreams.

~

I deserve respect, love, and recognition for my contributions.

~

My self-love grows stronger each day, nurturing my well-being.

~

I am open to learning and expanding my knowledge.

~

I am a resilient spirit, capable of overcoming any obstacle.

~

I am a woman of substance, with a powerful impact on the world.

∼

I trust in the divine timing of my life's unfolding.

∼

I release all fear and embrace the limitless possibilities before me.

∼

I am a queen, embracing the regality within my heritage and individuality.

∼

I am a beacon of melanin magic, radiating the beauty of my skin with pride.

∼

I am a creator of cultural richness, honoring and preserving the legacy of my ancestors.

∼

I am a vessel of resilience, embodying the strength and fortitude of black women.

∼

I am a magnet for positive representations, amplifying the diverse stories of black women.

～

I am a champion for self-love, celebrating the unique features that make me extraordinary.

～

I am a source of empowerment, uplifting fellow black women to recognize their brilliance.

～

I am a guardian of my roots, cultivating a deep connection to my African heritage.

～

I am a creator of unity, fostering sisterhood and solidarity among black women.

～

I am a beacon of authenticity, fearlessly expressing my true self with cultural pride.

～

I am a source of encouragement, inspiring other black women to pursue their dreams boldly.

~

I am a magnet for positive change, contributing to a world that embraces diversity and inclusion.

~

I am a champion for representation, advocating for the visibility and recognition of black women.

~

I am a vessel of wisdom, drawing strength from the resilience of black women who came before me.

~

I am a guardian of self-expression, using my voice to amplify the experiences of black women.

~

I am a creator of beauty, recognizing and celebrating the diversity of black beauty.

~

I am a source of empowerment, encouraging black women to embrace their natural essence.

~

I am a beacon of strength, navigating challenges with the grace and power inherent in black women.

～

I am a magnet for positive energy, attracting uplifting vibrations that resonate with my spirit.

～

I am a champion for self-care, recognizing the importance of nurturing my mind, body, and soul.

～

I am a beacon of strength, navigating challenges with grace and determination.

～

I am a source of clarity, making decisions that align with my highest good.

～

I am a magnet for positive connections, surrounding myself with uplifting souls.

～

I am a guardian of my thoughts, cultivating a mindset that empowers me.

∾

I am a creator of laughter, finding joy in the simple pleasures of life.

∾

I am a champion for growth, embracing opportunities for personal development.

∾

I am a magnet for positive energy, attracting good vibes into my life effortlessly.

∾

I am a beacon of resilience, bouncing back from setbacks with grace and strength.

∾

I am a source of encouragement, motivating myself and others to persevere.

∾

I am a creator of harmonious relationships, fostering understanding and connection.

∾

I am a guardian of my dreams, nurturing them with dedication and determination.

~

I am a magnet for creativity, expressing my unique ideas with confidence.

~

I am a champion for self-discovery, uncovering new aspects of myself every day.

~

I am a vessel of courage, stepping boldly into the unknown with faith.

~

I am a beacon of gratitude, appreciating the abundance that surrounds me.

~

I am a source of empowerment, inspiring those around me to believe in themselves.

~

I am a magnet for positive transformations, evolving into the best version of me.

∾

I am a guardian of my time, investing it in activities that align with my goals.

∾

I am a creator of abundance, recognizing the wealth of opportunities available to me.

∾

I am a champion for mindfulness, savoring the present moment with awareness.

∾

I am a vessel of kindness, extending compassion to myself and others.

∾

I am a beacon of trust, having faith in the journey and its unfolding.

∾

I am a magnet for love, cultivating deep and meaningful connections.

∾

I am a source of inspiration, sparking creativity and passion in those I encounter.

∼

I am a guardian of positivity, choosing optimism in every circumstance.

∼

I am a creator of balance, maintaining harmony in my mind, body, and soul.

∼

I am a champion for authenticity, embracing my true self authentically.

∼

I am a magnet for wisdom, learning valuable lessons from every experience.

∼

I am a vessel of serenity, finding peace within myself and my surroundings.

∼

I am a beacon of joy, radiating happiness to brighten the world around me.

~

I am a source of empowerment, uplifting others to recognize their strength.

~

I am a guardian of my well-being, prioritizing self-care in my daily life.

~

I am a creator of positive impact, contributing to the well-being of others.

~

I am a magnet for success, and I welcome achievements with open arms.

~

I am a champion for self-reflection, understanding, and evolving from within.

~

I am a vessel of hope, inspiring optimism and resilience in those I encounter.

~

I am a vessel of self-compassion, treating myself with kindness and understanding.

～

I am a magnet for abundance, attracting prosperity in all areas of my life.

～

I am a beacon of empowerment, inspiring others to embrace their potential.

～

I am a source of resilience, overcoming obstacles with unwavering strength.

～

I am a guardian of my energy, choosing to invest it in positive endeavors.

～

I am a creator of positive habits, fostering behaviors that support my well-being.

～

I am a magnet for serenity, finding peace amid life's fluctuations.

～

I am a champion for self-care, prioritizing activities that nurture my soul.

～

I am a vessel of gratitude, expressing thanks for both challenges and triumphs.

～

I am a beacon of authenticity, embracing my true self with love and acceptance.

～

I am a source of inspiration, igniting the spark of creativity in those around me.

～

I am a magnet for miracles, recognizing the extraordinary in everyday moments.

～

I am a guardian of my inner peace, creating boundaries that protect my tranquility.

～

I am a creator of positive change, contributing to a world filled with kindness.

～

I am a champion for self-expression, sharing my thoughts and feelings authentically.

～

I am a vessel of wisdom, learning and growing from every experience.

～

I am a beacon of love, radiating compassion to all beings.

～

I am a source of encouragement, uplifting others to pursue their dreams.

～

I am a magnet for success, achieving my goals with determination and focus.

～

I am a guardian of my dreams, nurturing them with passion and dedication.

~

I am a creator of joy, finding happiness in the journey as well as the destination.

~

I am a champion for balance, harmonizing the various aspects of my life.

~

I am a vessel of hope, inspiring optimism and resilience in those around me.

~

I am a beacon of kindness, spreading goodwill wherever I go.

~

I am a vessel of cultural pride, infusing every aspect of my life with the richness of my heritage.

~

I am a guardian of my dreams, pursuing my aspirations with the resilience of a black queen.

~

I am a creator of joy, finding delight in the beauty and vibrancy of black culture.

❧

I am a source of encouragement, supporting fellow black women in their endeavors.

❧

I am a magnet for success, breaking barriers and achieving greatness in my unique way.

❧

I am a beacon of confidence, embracing the power and grace that comes from being a black woman.

❧

I am a source of authenticity, living true to my roots and values as a black woman.

❧

I am a champion for inclusivity, creating spaces that celebrate and uplift black women.

❧

I am a vessel of resilience, drawing strength from the stories of triumph within the black community.

∾

I am a guardian of self-love, recognizing the beauty that exists in every shade of melanin.

∾

I am a creator of positive change, using my influence to uplift and empower black women.

∾

I am a magnet for love, surrounding myself with relationships that appreciate and honor my essence.

∾

I am a beacon of inspiration, encouraging black women to embrace their unique journey.

∾

I am a source of empowerment, recognizing the limitless potential within black women.

∾

I am a champion for self-expression, fearlessly expressing my identity as a black woman.

∾

I am a vessel of wisdom, carrying the ancestral knowledge and strength of black women.

∼

I am a guardian of cultural heritage, preserving and celebrating the traditions that define me.

∼

I am a creator of positive energy, infusing love and light into every interaction.

∼

I am a magnet for resilience, facing challenges with the enduring spirit of black women.

∼

I am a beacon of self-love, recognizing and celebrating the beauty within my melanin.

∼

I am a source of empowerment, encouraging black women to embrace their unique talents and gifts.

∼

I am a guardian of sisterhood, fostering connections and support within the black community.

∼

I am a creator of cultural appreciation, celebrating the richness and diversity of black heritage.

∼

I am a magnet for positive change, actively contributing to breaking down barriers and promoting equality.

∼

I am a champion for self-expression, expressing the multifaceted layers of my identity as a black woman.

∼

I am a vessel of strength, drawing inspiration from the resilience of black women who paved the way.

∼

I am a beacon of confidence, standing tall and proud in the beauty of my blackness.

∼

I am a source of encouragement, uplifting fellow black women to overcome obstacles and reach their goals.

∼

I am a magnet for opportunities, attracting pathways that honor and showcase the brilliance of black women.

～

I am a guardian of self-determination, charting my course with the knowledge that I am limitless.

～

I am a creator of positive narratives, contributing to a narrative that amplifies the achievements and successes of black women.

～

I am a source of empowerment, reminding black women of their inherent worth and capabilities.

～

I am a champion for authenticity, embracing and expressing the unique facets of being a black woman.

～

I am a vessel of cultural pride, embracing and sharing the traditions that make me who I am.

～

I am a beacon of resilience, weathering storms with the enduring strength passed down through generations.

∼

I am a magnet for love, creating spaces that cultivate love, respect, and understanding for black women.

∼

I am a guardian of dreams, encouraging black women to dream big and pursue their aspirations.

∼

I am a creator of positive impact, leaving a legacy that uplifts and inspires generations to come.

∼

I am a source of encouragement, supporting the dreams and ambitions of black women around me.

∼

I am a champion for self-love, recognizing that my love for myself is a powerful force that radiates outward.

∼

I am a vessel of empowerment, helping other black women recognize their strengths and potential.

∽

I am a beacon of inspiration, inspiring creativity, innovation, and excellence in the black community.

∽

I am a magnet for unity, fostering connections and solidarity among black women.

∽

I am a guardian of legacy, honoring the achievements and contributions of black women throughout history.

∽

I am a creator of joy, finding happiness in the celebration of my black identity.

∽

I am a source of encouragement, reminding black women that they are not alone in their journey.

∽

I am a champion for self-expression, expressing my unique voice and perspective as a black woman.

∽

I am a vessel of wisdom, tapping into the collective knowledge and resilience of black women.

~

I am a beacon of confidence, exuding self-assurance and pride in my capabilities.

~

I am a magnet for positive energy, attracting good vibes into my life effortlessly.

~

I am a beacon of resilience, bouncing back from setbacks with grace and strength.

~

I am a source of encouragement, motivating myself and others to persevere.

~

I am a creator of harmonious relationships, fostering understanding and connection.

~

I am a guardian of my dreams, nurturing them with dedication and determination.

≈

I am a magnet for creativity, expressing my unique ideas with confidence.

≈

I am a champion for self-discovery, uncovering new aspects of myself every day.

≈

I am a vessel of courage, stepping boldly into the unknown with faith.

≈

I am a beacon of gratitude, appreciating the abundance that surrounds me.

≈

I am a source of empowerment, inspiring those around me to believe in themselves.

≈

I am a magnet for positive transformations, evolving into the best version of me.

≈

I am a guardian of my time, investing it in activities that align with my goals.

∾

I am a creator of abundance, recognizing the wealth of opportunities available to me.

∾

I am a champion for mindfulness, savoring the present moment with awareness.

∾

I am a vessel of kindness, extending compassion to myself and others.

∾

I am a beacon of trust, having faith in the journey and its unfolding.

∾

I am a magnet for love, cultivating deep and meaningful connections.

∾

I am a source of inspiration, sparking creativity and passion in those I encounter.

∼

I am a guardian of positivity, choosing optimism in every circumstance.

∼

I am a creator of balance, maintaining harmony in my mind, body, and soul.

∼

I am a champion for authenticity, embracing my true self authentically.

∼

I am a magnet for wisdom, learning valuable lessons from every experience.

∼

I am a vessel of serenity, finding peace within myself and my surroundings.

∼

I am a beacon of joy, radiating happiness to brighten the world around me.

∼

I am a source of empowerment, uplifting others to recognize their strength.

∼

I am a guardian of my well-being, prioritizing self-care in my daily life.

∼

I am a creator of positive impact, contributing to the well-being of others.

∼

I am a magnet for success, and I welcome achievements with open arms.

∼

I am a vessel of hope, inspiring optimism and resilience in those I encounter.

∼

I am a beacon of strength, navigating challenges with grace and determination.

∼

I am a source of clarity, making decisions that align with my highest good.

∼

I am a magnet for positive connections, surrounding myself with uplifting souls.

∼

I am a guardian of my thoughts, cultivating a mindset that empowers me.

∼

I am a creator of laughter, finding joy in the simple pleasures of life.

∼

I am a champion for growth, embracing opportunities for personal development.

∼

I am a vessel of self-compassion, treating myself with kindness and understanding.

∼

I am a magnet for abundance, attracting prosperity in all areas of my life.

∼

I am a beacon of empowerment, inspiring others to embrace their potential.

∼

I am a source of resilience, overcoming obstacles with unwavering strength.

∼

I am a source of empowerment, recognizing and celebrating the diversity within the black community.

∼

I am a magnet for positive energy, attracting love, light, and positivity into my life.

∼

I am a guardian of self-expression, embracing the beauty of my unique voice and perspective.

∼

I am a creator of cultural fusion, blending traditions and innovations that honor my heritage.

∼

I am a beacon of strength, standing resilient in the face of challenges, a testament to the power of black women.

~

I am a source of encouragement, fostering a community where black women uplift and support each other.

~

I am a champion for authenticity, unapologetically showcasing the multifaceted layers of my identity.

~

I am a vessel of empowerment, inspiring black women to recognize their individual and collective power.

~

I am a magnet for success, achieving greatness and breaking barriers in my chosen endeavors.

~

I am a guardian of self-love, cultivating a deep and unshakeable love for myself in all my uniqueness.

~

I am a creator of positive narratives, sharing stories that celebrate the triumphs and resilience of black women.

~

I am a source of encouragement, reminding black women that their dreams are valid and achievable.

∿

I am a champion for inclusivity, working towards creating spaces that embrace and celebrate diversity.

∿

I am a beacon of wisdom, tapping into the ancestral knowledge and wisdom passed down through generations.

∿

I am a magnet for unity, fostering connections and sisterhood among black women worldwide.

∿

I am a guardian of self-determination, forging my path with purpose and determination.

∿

I am a creator of joy, finding happiness in the beauty of black culture and the richness of my experiences.

∿

I am a source of empowerment, encouraging black women to use their voices to create positive change.

∾

I am a champion for self-expression, expressing my identity boldly and unapologetically.

∾

I am a vessel of resilience, embodying the spirit of black women who have overcome adversity.

∾

I am a beacon of love, radiating love and compassion to myself and those around me.

∾

I am a magnet for positive change, actively contributing to dismantling systemic barriers and promoting equality.

∾

I am a guardian of dreams, nurturing the aspirations of black women and helping them flourish.

∾

I am a creator of cultural appreciation, fostering an environment that values and honors diverse backgrounds.

∾

I am a source of encouragement, uplifting black women to shine brightly in their unique brilliance.

∾

I am a champion for authenticity, expressing my true self with confidence and grace.

∾

I am a guardian of my energy, choosing to invest it in positive endeavors.

∾

I am a creator of positive habits, fostering behaviors that support my well-being.

∾

I am a champion for self-care, prioritizing activities that nurture my soul.

∾

I am a vessel of gratitude, expressing thanks for both challenges and triumphs.

≈

I am a beacon of authenticity, embracing my true self with love and acceptance.

≈

I am a source of inspiration, igniting the spark of creativity in those around me.

≈

I am a magnet for miracles, recognizing the extraordinary in everyday moments.

≈

I am a guardian of my inner peace, creating boundaries that protect my tranquility.

≈

I am a creator of positive change, contributing to a world filled with kindness.

≈

I am a champion for self-expression, sharing my thoughts and feelings authentically.

~

I am a vessel of wisdom, learning and growing from every experience.

~

I am a beacon of love, radiating compassion to all beings.

~

I am a source of encouragement, uplifting others to pursue their dreams.

~

I am a magnet for success, achieving my goals with determination and focus.

~

I am a guardian of my dreams, nurturing them with passion and dedication.

~

I am a creator of joy, finding happiness in the journey as well as the destination.

~

I am a champion for balance, harmonizing the various aspects of my life.

~

I am a vessel of hope, inspiring optimism and resilience in those around me.

~

I am a beacon of kindness, spreading goodwill wherever I go.

~

I am a source of empowerment, recognizing the strength within myself.

~

I am a magnet for positive opportunities, attracting them with an open heart.

~

I am a guardian of my boundaries, honoring and preserving my well-being.

~

I am a creator of beauty, appreciating the elegance in both simple and complex moments.

~

I am a champion for perseverance, persisting in the face of challenges.

~

I am a vessel of acceptance, embracing all aspects of myself without judgment.

~

I am a beacon of wisdom, making choices aligned with my higher self.

~

I am a source of inspiration, sparking motivation in those around me.

~

I am a magnet for vibrant health, nourishing my body, mind, and spirit.

~

I am a guardian of my focus, directing my attention to what truly matters.

~

I am a creator of positive vibrations, uplifting the energy
of my surroundings.

～

I am a champion for kindness, extending compassion to
myself and others.

～

I am a vessel of joy, cultivating an atmosphere of
happiness in my life.

～

I am a beacon of confidence, trusting in my abilities and
embracing my uniqueness.

～

I am a source of encouragement, fostering a supportive
environment for growth.

～

I am a magnet for abundance, attracting prosperity and
success effortlessly.

～

I am a guardian of my dreams, pursuing them with
unwavering dedication.

∼

I am a creator of peace, fostering harmony within and around me.

∼

I am a champion for self-love, recognizing and appreciating my worth.

∼

I am a beacon of gratitude, expressing thanks for the abundance in my life.

∼

I am a vessel of empowerment, recognizing that the power within me contributes to the collective strength of black women.

∼

I am a beacon of inspiration, igniting passion and creativity within the hearts of fellow black women.

∼

I am a magnet for unity, working towards building bridges and connections within the black community.

∼

I am a guardian of resilience, drawing strength from the legacy of black women who have paved the way.

∾

I am a creator of positive impact, leaving a lasting legacy that inspires generations to come.

∾

I am a source of encouragement, inspiring black women to embrace their uniqueness and shine in their authentic glory.

∾

I am a champion for self-love, recognizing the divine beauty within me and celebrating it with unapologetic pride.

∾

I am a vessel of empowerment, helping black women recognize their worth and supporting them in their journey.

∾

I am a beacon of strength, breaking through barriers and paving the way for future generations of black women.

∾

I am a magnet for positive connections, building networks that empower and uplift black women in various fields.

∼

I am a guardian of heritage, preserving and sharing the rich tapestry of black history and culture.

∼

I am a creator of joy, finding delight in the vibrant expressions of art, music, and creativity within the black community.

∼

I am a source of encouragement, reminding black women that their voices are powerful and deserve to be heard.

∼

I am a champion for resilience, embodying the unwavering spirit of black women who have overcome adversity.

∼

I am a vessel of wisdom, embracing the teachings and lessons passed down through generations.

∼

I am a beacon of love, promoting self-love and love for others as foundational elements of personal growth.

～

I am a magnet for positivity, attracting opportunities that align with my vision for a better, brighter future.

～

I am a guardian of dreams, fostering an environment where black women can dream big and pursue their passions.

～

I am a creator of cultural pride, instilling a deep sense of pride and love for the diverse black heritage.

～

I am a source of encouragement, supporting black women to take up spaces and excel in various industries.

～

I am a champion for inclusivity, creating spaces that value and celebrate the unique perspectives of black women.

～

I am a vessel of empowerment, using my influence to uplift and amplify the voices of black women.

～

I am a beacon of inspiration, sparking creativity and innovation within the hearts of black women.

～

I am a magnet for unity, fostering collaborations and alliances that strengthen the bonds within the black community.

～

I am a guardian of resilience, drawing strength from the stories of black women who stood tall in the face of challenges.

～

I am a creator of positive impact, contributing to a world where black women's contributions are recognized and celebrated.

～

I am a source of encouragement, reminding black women that their aspirations are valid and attainable.

～

I am a champion for self-expression, expressing the unique facets of my identity fearlessly and authentically.

~

I am a vessel of empowerment, recognizing that my success contributes to the collective empowerment of black women.

~

I am a beacon of inspiration, inspiring black women to pursue their passions and live authentically.

~

I am a magnet for unity, fostering a sense of sisterhood and collaboration within the black community.

~

I am a guardian of dreams, encouraging black women to dream big and pursue their goals with determination.

~

I am a creator of cultural appreciation, celebrating the diversity and richness of black cultures worldwide.

~

I am a source of encouragement, uplifting black women to overcome challenges and thrive in every aspect of life.

~

I am a champion for self-love, embracing my unique beauty and encouraging others to do the same.

~

I am a vessel of empowerment, using my influence to advocate for justice, equality, and positive change.

~

I am a beacon of strength, standing tall and resilient in the face of societal challenges and stereotypes.

~

I am a magnet for community, fostering connections and collaboration to uplift the black community.

~

I am a guardian of history, preserving and sharing the stories of black women who have shaped the course of history.

~

I am a creator of joy, infusing laughter, celebration, and vibrancy into every corner of my life.

～

I am a source of encouragement, inspiring black women to embrace their ambitions fearlessly.

～

I am a champion for self-awareness, continuously exploring and understanding the depths of my identity.

～

I am a vessel of inspiration, encouraging black women to explore their creativity and express their unique talents.

～

I am a beacon of love, promoting love and unity within the black community and beyond.

～

I am a magnet for progress, actively contributing to advancements that benefit black women.

～

I am a guardian of resilience, drawing strength from the powerful legacy of black women who forged paths.

∼

I am a creator of cultural fusion, bridging the gaps between diverse black cultures and celebrating their interconnectedness.

∼

I am a source of encouragement, reminding black women of the transformative power they hold within.

∼

I am a champion for self-acceptance, embracing every part of myself with love and appreciation.

∼

I am a vessel of empowerment, lifting others as I rise, ensuring that no one is left behind.

∼

I am a beacon of inspiration, lighting the way for future generations of black women.

∼

I am a magnet for unity, fostering collaborations that amplify the collective strength of black women.

∼

I am a guardian of dreams, encouraging black women to pursue their passions with determination.

~

I am a creator of cultural appreciation, weaving the threads of diverse black cultures into a tapestry of beauty.

I am a source of encouragement, supporting black women to break barriers and excel in every field.

~

I am a champion for self-expression, embracing the power of my voice and the uniqueness of my story.

~

I am a vessel of empowerment, recognizing the importance of uplifting and supporting one another.

~

I am a beacon of resilience, standing firm against adversity and inspiring others to do the same.

~

I am a magnet for positive change, actively working towards dismantling systemic inequalities.

~

I am a guardian of heritage, preserving and passing down the cultural richness of black traditions.

∾

I am a creator of joy, finding happiness in the celebration of black excellence and achievements.

∾

I am a source of encouragement, inspiring black women to pursue education, knowledge, and personal growth.

∾

I am a champion for self-love, recognizing that my worth extends beyond societal standards.

∾

I am a vessel of empowerment, using my skills and talents to uplift and inspire those around me.

∾

I am a beacon of inspiration, sparking creativity and innovation within the black community.

∾

I am a magnet for unity, fostering connections and alliances that strengthen the bonds within the black community.

~

I am a guardian of resilience, drawing strength from the stories of black women who stood tall in the face of challenges.

~

I am a beacon of gratitude, appreciating the present moment and all its blessings.

~

I am a magnet for positive outcomes, attracting success effortlessly.

~

I am a guardian of my joy, choosing happiness in every circumstance.

~

I am a creator of positive habits, cultivating behaviors that support my well-being.

~

I am a vessel of resilience, overcoming challenges with unwavering strength.

~

I am a source of kindness, spreading compassion wherever I go.

~

I am a champion for self-growth, evolving into a better version of myself every day.

~

I am a magnet for prosperity, attracting abundance in all areas of my life.

~

I am a beacon of positivity, radiating good vibes to those around me.

~

I am a guardian of my time, investing it in activities that align with my goals.

~

I am a creator of beauty, recognizing and celebrating the beauty within and around me.

~

I am a source of inspiration, inspiring others to embrace
their uniqueness.

~

I am a magnet for positive connections, attracting
supportive relationships.

~

I am a champion for self-belief, trusting in my abilities
and potential.

~

I am a beacon of love, sharing love generously with myself
and others.

~

I am a guardian of my dreams, pursuing them with
passion and dedication.

~

I am a creator of positive change, contributing to a world
filled with kindness.

~

I am a source of encouragement, uplifting those who may need a guiding light.

~

I am a magnet for miracles, acknowledging the magic in everyday moments.

~

I am a champion for authenticity, embracing my true self with authenticity.

~

I am a vessel of wisdom, learning from every experience life presents.

~

I am a beacon of confidence, standing tall in my uniqueness and capabilities.

~

I am a source of light, illuminating the world with positivity and kindness.

~

I am a magnet for meaningful connections, forging bonds that nourish my soul.

~

I am a guardian of resilience, bouncing back from
challenges stronger than ever.

~

I am a creator of harmony, balancing the various aspects
of my life with grace.

~

I am a vessel of empowerment, empowering myself and
others to reach new heights.

~

I am a beacon of inspiration, sparking creativity in those
around me.

~

I am a magnet for good fortune, attracting blessings into
my life.

~

I am a champion for self-compassion, treating myself
with gentleness and love.

~

I am a guardian of my thoughts, ensuring they align with positivity and growth.

≈

I am a creator of positive energy, infusing optimism into every situation.

≈

I am a source of motivation, propelling myself forward with determination.

≈

I am a magnet for success, achieving my goals with focus and perseverance.

≈

I am a beacon of wisdom, learning and evolving from every experience.

≈

I am a vessel of gratitude, expressing appreciation for the beauty of life.

≈

I am a champion for authenticity, embracing my true self fearlessly.

~

I am a magnet for abundance, attracting prosperity in all areas of my life.

~

I am a guardian of my well-being, prioritizing self-care as a sacred practice.

~

I am a creator of joy, finding delight in both small and significant moments.

~

I am a source of encouragement, uplifting those who need support.

~

I am a beacon of kindness, extending compassion to myself and others.

~

I am a magnet for positive transformations, evolving into the best version of myself.

~

I am a champion for self-expression, fearlessly sharing my voice with the world.

∾

I am a vessel of courage, facing challenges with resilience and bravery.

∾

I am a guardian of my dreams, nurturing them with unwavering dedication.

∾

I am a creator of serenity, finding peace within the depths of my being.

∾

I am a source of empowerment, recognizing the strength within me.

∾

I am a magnet for love, both giving and receiving it abundantly.

∾

I am a beacon of hope, inspiring optimism and faith in the hearts of others.

~

I am a champion for balance, harmonizing the different aspects of my life.

~

I am a vessel of authenticity, honoring and expressing my true self.

~

I am a guardian of positivity, choosing optimism in every circumstance.

~

I am a creator of clarity, making decisions aligned with my highest good.

~

I am a magnet for positive vibrations, elevating the energy around me.

~

I am a source of strength, tapping into my inner power with confidence.

~

I am a champion for self-love, embracing myself with compassion and acceptance.

~

I am a source of empowerment, empowering myself and others to thrive.

~

I am a guardian of my inner peace, creating a sanctuary of tranquility within.

~

I am a creator of joy, finding delight in both ordinary and extraordinary moments.

~

I am a magnet for clarity, seeing opportunities and solutions with a clear mind.

~

I am a champion for self-care, prioritizing activities that nourish my mind, body, and soul.

~

I am a vessel of gratitude, expressing thanks for the journey and its lessons.

∾

I am a beacon of inspiration, igniting the spark of creativity in those around me.

∾

I am a source of empowerment, recognizing and embracing my personal power.

∾

I am a magnet for positive energy, infusing optimism into every interaction.

∾

I am a guardian of my potential, unlocking new possibilities with each step.

∾

I am a creator of peace, bringing calmness and tranquility to my surroundings.

∾

I am a champion for resilience, bouncing back from challenges stronger than ever.

∾

I am a creator of positive impact, contributing to a world where black women's contributions are recognized and celebrated.

∼

I am a source of encouragement, reminding black women that their aspirations are valid and attainable.

∼

I am a champion for self-expression, expressing the unique facets of my identity fearlessly and authentically.

∼

I am a vessel of empowerment, recognizing that my success contributes to the collective empowerment of black women.

∼

I am a beacon of inspiration, inspiring black women to pursue their passions and live authentically.

∼

I am a magnet for unity, fostering a sense of sisterhood and collaboration within the black community.

∼

I am a guardian of dreams, encouraging black women to dream big and pursue their goals with determination.

~

I am a creator of cultural appreciation, celebrating the diversity and richness of black cultures worldwide.

~

I am a source of encouragement, uplifting black women to overcome challenges and thrive in every aspect of life.

~

I am a champion for self-love, embracing my unique beauty and encouraging others to do the same.

~

I am a vessel of empowerment, using my influence to advocate for justice, equality, and positive change.

~

I am a beacon of strength, standing tall and resilient in the face of societal challenges and stereotypes.

~

I am a magnet for community, fostering connections and collaboration to uplift the black community.

∾

I am a guardian of history, preserving and sharing the stories of black women who have shaped the course of history.

∾

I am a creator of joy, infusing laughter, celebration, and vibrancy into every corner of my life.

∾

I am a source of encouragement, inspiring black women to embrace their ambitions fearlessly.

∾

I am a champion for self-awareness, continuously exploring and understanding the depths of my identity.

∾

I am a vessel of inspiration, encouraging black women to explore their creativity and express their unique talents.

∾

I am a beacon of love, promoting love and unity within the black community and beyond.

∾

I am a magnet for progress, actively contributing to advancements that benefit black women.

∼

I am a guardian of resilience, drawing strength from the powerful legacy of black women who forged paths.

∼

I am a creator of cultural fusion, bridging the gaps between diverse black cultures and celebrating their interconnectedness.

∼

I am a beacon of strength, navigating challenges with grace and determination.

∼

I am a source of compassion, extending understanding and empathy to myself and others.

∼

I am a magnet for positive transformations, evolving into the best version of myself.

∼

I am a guardian of my energy, choosing to surround myself with positivity.

∾

I am a creator of abundance, attracting prosperity in both expected and unexpected ways.

∾

I am a vessel of inspiration, inspiring others to believe in their dreams.

∾

I am a champion for self-love, recognizing my worthiness and embracing my uniqueness.

∾

I am a magnet for good health, nurturing my body, mind, and spirit.

∾

I am a beacon of gratitude, finding joy in expressing thanks for life's blessings.

∾

I am a source of encouragement, uplifting those who may need a supportive word.

~

I am a guardian of my dreams, pursuing them with passion and resilience.

~

I am a creator of joy, infusing happiness into my daily experiences.

~

I am a magnet for positive relationships, attracting connections that uplift and inspire.

~

I am a champion for mindfulness, savoring each moment with presence and awareness.

~

I am a vessel of wisdom, gaining valuable insights from every life lesson.

~

I am a beacon of positivity, radiating optimism even in challenging times.

~

I am a source of empowerment, recognizing the strength within me.

∿

I am a magnet for love, attracting genuine and fulfilling connections.

∿

I am a guardian of my peace, choosing tranquility over stress and chaos.

∿

I am a creator of resilience, bouncing back from setbacks with unwavering determination.

∿

I am a champion for self-reflection, understanding and growing from my experiences.

∿

I am a magnet for opportunities, attracting doors that lead to success and fulfillment.

∿

I am a vessel of self-discovery, embracing the journey of understanding myself.

~

I am a beacon of authenticity, living true to myself and my values.

~

I am a source of kindness, extending compassion to all beings.

~

I am a guardian of my thoughts, cultivating a positive and empowering mindset.

~

I am a creator of beauty, finding and appreciating the beauty in both myself and others.

~

I am a magnet for positive energy, attracting good vibes into my life.

~

I am a champion for self-compassion, treating myself with gentleness and understanding.

~

I am a vessel of growth, evolving and expanding in all aspects of my life.

~

I am a source of encouragement, reminding black women of the transformative power they hold within.

~

I am a champion for self-acceptance, embracing every part of myself with love and appreciation.

~

I am a vessel of empowerment, lifting others as I rise, ensuring that no one is left behind.

~

I am a beacon of inspiration, lighting the way for future generations of black women.

~

I am a magnet for unity, fostering collaborations that amplify the collective strength of black women.

~

I am a guardian of dreams, encouraging black women to pursue their passions with determination.

∾

I am a creator of cultural appreciation, weaving the threads of diverse black cultures into a tapestry of beauty.

∾

I am a source of encouragement, supporting black women to break barriers and excel in every field.

∾

I am a beacon of courage, fearlessly embracing new opportunities and challenges.

∾

I am a source of encouragement, motivating myself and others to pursue greatness.

∾

I am a magnet for positive energy, attracting optimism and enthusiasm into my life.

∾

I am a guardian of my dreams, nurturing them with dedication and perseverance.

∾

I am a creator of positive change, contributing to a world filled with kindness.

~

I am a vessel of resilience, bouncing back from setbacks with unwavering strength.

~

I am a champion for self-belief, trusting in my abilities and potential.

~

I am a source of empowerment, recognizing the strength within me.

~

I am a magnet for love, both giving and receiving it abundantly.

~

I am a beacon of hope, inspiring optimism and faith in the hearts of others.

~

I am a guardian of balance, harmonizing the various aspects of my life.

~

I am a creator of clarity, making decisions with a focused and clear mind.

~

I am a vessel of gratitude, expressing thanks for the abundance in my life.

~

I am a champion for authenticity, embracing my true self with love and acceptance.

~

I am a magnet for prosperity, attracting wealth and abundance into my life.

~

I am a source of inspiration, sparking creativity and passion in those I encounter.

~

I am a guardian of positivity, choosing optimism in every circumstance.

~

I am a creator of balance, maintaining harmony in my mind, body, and soul.

≈

I am a beacon of wisdom, continuously learning and growing from life's experiences.

≈

I am a vessel of kindness, extending compassion to myself and others.

≈

I am a champion for self-care, prioritizing activities that nurture my well-being.

≈

I am a magnet for positive connections, surrounding myself with supportive individuals.

≈

I am a creator of joy, finding delight in both small and significant moments.

≈

I am a source of empowerment, uplifting others to recognize their strength.

~

I am a guardian of my well-being, nurturing my body, mind, and spirit.

~

I am a creator of positive impact, contributing to the well-being of others.

~

I am a magnet for success, and I welcome achievements with open arms.

~

I am a champion for self-reflection, understanding and evolving from within.

~

I am a vessel of hope, inspiring optimism and resilience in those I encounter.

~

I am a beacon of strength, navigating challenges with grace and determination.

~

I am a source of clarity, making decisions that align with my highest good.

~

I am a magnet for positive connections, surrounding myself with uplifting souls.

~

I am a guardian of my thoughts, cultivating a mindset that empowers me.

~

I am a creator of laughter, finding joy in the simple pleasures of life.

~

I am a champion for growth, embracing opportunities for personal development.

~

I am a vessel of self-compassion, treating myself with kindness and understanding.

~

I am a magnet for abundance, attracting prosperity in all areas of my life.

∽

I am a beacon of empowerment, inspiring those around me to thrive.

∽

I am a source of resilience, overcoming obstacles with unwavering strength.

∽

I am a guardian of my energy, choosing to invest it in positive endeavors.

∽

I am a champion for self-expression, embracing the power of my voice and the uniqueness of my story.

∽

I am a vessel of empowerment, recognizing the importance of uplifting and supporting one another.

∽

I am a beacon of resilience, standing firm against adversity and inspiring others to do the same.

∽

I am a magnet for positive change, actively working towards dismantling systemic inequalities.

≈

I am a guardian of heritage, preserving and passing down the cultural richness of black traditions.

≈

I am a creator of joy, finding happiness in the celebration of black excellence and achievements.

≈

I am a source of encouragement, inspiring black women to pursue education, knowledge, and personal growth.

≈

I am a champion for self-love, recognizing that my worth extends beyond societal standards.

≈

I am a vessel of empowerment, using my skills and talents to uplift and inspire those around me.

≈

I am a beacon of inspiration, sparking creativity and innovation within the black community.

∽

I am a magnet for unity, fostering connections and alliances that strengthen the bonds within the black community.

∽

I am a guardian of resilience, drawing strength from the stories of black women who stood tall in the face of challenges.

∽

I am a creator of positive impact, contributing to a world where black women's contributions are recognized and celebrated.

∽

I am a source of encouragement, reminding black women that their aspirations are valid and attainable.

∽

I am a champion for self-expression, expressing the unique facets of my identity fearlessly and authentically.

∽

I am a vessel of empowerment, recognizing that my success contributes to the collective empowerment of black women.

∾

I am a beacon of inspiration, inspiring black women to pursue their passions and live authentically.

∾

I am a magnet for unity, fostering a sense of sisterhood and collaboration within the black community.

∾

I am a guardian of dreams, encouraging black women to dream big and pursue their goals with determination.

∾

I am a creator of cultural appreciation, celebrating the diversity and richness of black cultures worldwide.

∾

I am a source of encouragement, uplifting black women to overcome challenges and thrive in every aspect of life.

∾

I am a champion for self-love, embracing my unique beauty and encouraging others to do the same.

∽

I am a vessel of strength, channeling the resilience and fortitude of my ancestors into my daily life.

∽

I am a beacon of cultural celebration, honoring the traditions and rituals that connect me to my roots.

∽

I am a magnet for positive change, actively participating in movements that uplift and empower black communities.

∽

I am a guardian of education, continuously seeking knowledge and sharing it to inspire the next generation.

∽

I am a creator of inclusivity, fostering spaces that appreciate and embrace the diversity within the black diaspora.

∽

I am a source of encouragement, uplifting black women to embrace their passions and pursue their dreams.

~

I am a champion for self-empowerment, recognizing that my journey contributes to the collective strength of black women.

~

I am a vessel of authenticity, unapologetically expressing my true self in a world that celebrates my uniqueness.

~

I am a beacon of inspiration, sparking creativity and innovation within the black community.

~

I am a magnet for unity, weaving connections that amplify the collective voice and impact of black women.

~

I am a guardian of dreams, encouraging black women to dream boldly and fearlessly.

~

I am a creator of cultural awareness, promoting understanding and appreciation for the diversity within the black experience.

~

I am a source of encouragement, reminding black women that their resilience is a force to be reckoned with.

~

I am a champion for self-love, recognizing that my worth is inherent and not determined by external standards.

~

I am a vessel of empowerment, extending a helping hand to uplift those who may need support.

~

I am a beacon of wisdom, tapping into the wealth of knowledge within the black community.

~

I am a magnet for positive vibrations, attracting joy and abundance into every aspect of my life.

~

I am a guardian of self-expression, encouraging black women to use their voices to inspire and create change.

~

I am a creator of joy, finding happiness in the celebration of black culture and accomplishments.

~

I am a source of encouragement, fostering a spirit of sisterhood and support among black women.

~

I am a champion for self-determination, carving my path with resilience and determination.

~

I am a vessel of cultural pride, embracing and showcasing the beauty of black heritage.

~

I am a beacon of love, radiating love and compassion to myself and others.

~

I am a magnet for positive connections, building relationships that empower and uplift those around me.

∼

I am a guardian of resilience, standing strong in the face of challenges and inspiring others to do the same.

∼

I am a creator of positive impact, leaving a legacy that paves the way for future generations.

∼

I am a source of encouragement, reminding black women of their inherent strength and capabilities.

∼

I am a champion for self-expression, expressing my unique voice and perspective with confidence.

∼

I am a vessel of empowerment, using my influence to advocate for equity and justice.

∼

I am a beacon of inspiration, lighting the way for others to follow their dreams fearlessly.

∼

I am a magnet for unity, building bridges and connections that strengthen the bonds within the black community.

∼

I am a guardian of resilience, drawing strength from the rich history of black women who defied the odds.

∼

I am a creator of positive change, actively contributing to a world where everyone is seen, heard, and valued.

∼

I am a source of encouragement, uplifting black women to embrace their authenticity and shine brightly.

∼

I am a champion for self-love, recognizing the beauty in my individuality and radiating that love outward.

∼

I am a vessel of empowerment, using my influence to inspire and uplift those around me.

∼

I am a beacon of resilience, navigating challenges with grace and strength, a testament to the indomitable spirit of black women.

~

I am a magnet for positive energy, radiating a vibrant aura that uplifts and inspires those in my presence.

~

I am a guardian of legacy, honoring the trailblazing black women who paved the way for progress and change.

~

I am a creator of cultural fusion, embracing the richness of diversity within the black community.

~

I am a source of encouragement, uplifting black women to break barriers and excel in every arena.

~

I am a champion for self-expression, expressing my truth boldly and authentically, contributing to the mosaic of black voices.

~

I am a vessel of empowerment, using my influence to create spaces where black women thrive and succeed.

~

I am a beacon of inspiration, igniting passion and purpose in the hearts of those around me.

~

I am a magnet for unity, fostering collaborations that amplify the collective strength of black women globally.

~

I am a guardian of dreams, encouraging black women to dream limitlessly and pursue their aspirations with determination.

~

I am a creator of cultural appreciation, celebrating the beauty of diverse black cultures and traditions.

~

I am a source of encouragement, reminding black women that their stories are powerful and worthy of being told.

~

I am a champion for self-acceptance, embracing every facet of my identity with love and unshakeable confidence.

∿

I am a vessel of empowerment, sharing knowledge and resources to uplift the black community.

∿

I am a beacon of wisdom, tapping into the ancestral knowledge and resilience passed down through generations.

∿

I am a magnet for positive change, actively participating in initiatives that dismantle systemic injustices.

∿

I am a guardian of heritage, preserving and promoting the rich cultural tapestry of black history.

∿

I am a creator of joy, finding delight in the celebration of black achievements and contributions.

∿

I am a source of encouragement, fostering a culture of support and sisterhood among black women.

~

I am a champion for self-empowerment, recognizing that my journey adds to the legacy of empowered black women.

~

I am a vessel of authenticity, fearlessly showcasing my true self in a world that cherishes diversity.

~

I am a beacon of love, spreading compassion and kindness to create a world filled with understanding.

~

I am a magnet for positive connections, building networks that amplify the impact of black women in various fields.

~

I am a guardian of resilience, drawing strength from the collective resilience and triumphs of black women.

~

I am a creator of positive impact, leaving a mark that contributes to a more equitable and inclusive future.

≈

I am a source of encouragement, reminding black women of their worthiness, brilliance, and limitless potential.

≈

I am a champion for self-expression, using my voice to challenge stereotypes and uplift the diverse narratives of black women.

≈

I am a vessel of empowerment, advocating for equal opportunities and representation for black women in all spheres.

≈

I am a beacon of inspiration, lighting the way for future generations of black women to dream, achieve, and soar.

≈

I am a magnet for unity, fostering a sense of belonging and camaraderie among black women worldwide.

≈

I am a guardian of dreams, inspiring black women to pursue their passions boldly and unapologetically.

~

I am a creator of cultural appreciation, recognizing the richness and beauty of black heritage in all its forms.

~

I am a source of encouragement, uplifting black women to embrace their unique journeys and celebrate their successes.

~

I am a champion for self-love, recognizing that my love for self is a powerful force that radiates positive energy.

~

I am a vessel of empowerment, using my talents and skills to uplift and inspire others in the black community.

~

I am a beacon of inspiration, encouraging black women to embrace their individuality and shine brightly.

~

I am a magnet for unity, fostering connections and collaborations that strengthen the collective power of black women.

∾

I am a guardian of resilience, drawing strength from the stories of black women who triumphed over adversity.

∾

I am a creator of positive change, actively contributing to dismantling systemic barriers and promoting equity.

∾

I am a source of encouragement, reminding black women that their dreams are valid, attainable, and deserving of pursuit.

∾

I am a champion for self-expression, fearlessly expressing my creativity and uniqueness as a black woman.

∾

I am a vessel of empowerment, using my skills and talents to uplift and inspire those around me.

∾

I am a beacon of inspiration, sparking creativity and innovation within the black community.

~

I am a magnet for unity, fostering connections and alliances that strengthen the bonds within the black community.

~

I am a guardian of resilience, drawing strength from the stories of black women who stood tall in the face of challenges.

~

I am a creator of positive impact, contributing to a world where black women's contributions are recognized and celebrated.

~

I am a source of encouragement, reminding black women that their aspirations are valid and attainable.

~

I am a champion for self-expression, expressing the unique facets of my identity fearlessly and authentically.

~

I am a vessel of empowerment, recognizing that my success contributes to the collective empowerment of black women.

~

I am a beacon of inspiration, inspiring black women to pursue their passions and live authentically.

~

I am a magnet for unity, fostering a sense of sisterhood and collaboration within the black community.

~

I am a guardian of dreams, encouraging black women to dream big and pursue their goals with determination.

~

I am a creator of cultural appreciation, celebrating the diversity and richness of black cultures worldwide.

~

I am a source of encouragement, uplifting black women to overcome challenges and thrive in every aspect of life.

~

I am a champion for self-love, embracing my unique beauty and encouraging others to do the same.

~

I am a vessel of empowerment, using my influence to advocate for justice, equality, and positive change.

~

I am a beacon of strength, standing tall and resilient in the face of societal challenges and stereotypes.

~

I am a magnet for community, fostering connections and collaboration to uplift the black community.

~

I am a guardian of history, preserving and sharing the stories of black women who have shaped the course of history.

~

I am a creator of joy, infusing laughter, celebration, and vibrancy into every corner of my life.

~

I am a source of encouragement, inspiring black women to embrace their ambitions fearlessly.

~

I am a champion for self-awareness, continuously exploring and understanding the depths of my identity.

~

I am a vessel of inspiration, encouraging black women to explore their creativity and express their unique talents.

~

I am a beacon of love, promoting love and unity within the black community and beyond.

~

I am a magnet for progress, actively contributing to advancements that benefit black women.

~

I am a guardian of resilience, drawing strength from the powerful legacy of black women who forged paths.

~

I am a creator of cultural fusion, bridging the gaps between diverse black cultures and celebrating their interconnectedness.

∼

I am a source of encouragement, reminding black women of the transformative power they hold within.

∼

I am a champion for self-acceptance, embracing every part of myself with love and appreciation.

∼

I am a vessel of empowerment, lifting others as I rise, ensuring that no one is left behind.

∼

I am a beacon of inspiration, lighting the way for future generations of black women.

∼

I am a magnet for unity, fostering collaborations that amplify the collective strength of black women.

∼

I am a guardian of dreams, encouraging black women to pursue their passions with determination.

~

I am a creator of cultural appreciation, weaving the threads of diverse black cultures into a tapestry of beauty.

~

I am a source of encouragement, supporting black women to break barriers and excel in every field.

~

I am a champion for self-expression, embracing the power of my voice and the uniqueness of my story.

~

I am a vessel of empowerment, recognizing the importance of uplifting and supporting one another.

~

I am a beacon of resilience, standing firm against adversity and inspiring others to do the same.

~

I am a magnet for positive change, actively working towards dismantling systemic inequalities.

∼

I am a guardian of heritage, preserving and passing down the cultural richness of black traditions.

∼

I am a creator of joy, finding happiness in the celebration of black excellence and achievements.

∼

I am a source of encouragement, inspiring black women to pursue education, knowledge, and personal growth.

∼

I am a champion for self-love, recognizing that my worth extends beyond societal standards.

∼

I am a vessel of empowerment, using my influence to uplift and inspire those around me.

∼

I am a beacon of inspiration, sparking creativity and innovation within the black community.

∼

I am a beacon of authenticity, embracing my uniqueness and expressing myself freely.

∼

I am a source of inspiration, inspiring others to tap into their creativity and passions.

∼

I am a guardian of my inner peace, cultivating a serene space within myself.

∼

I am a creator of joy, finding happiness in the simple pleasures of life.

∼

I am a magnet for positive energy, attracting good vibes into my life effortlessly.

∼

I am a champion for self-compassion, treating myself with kindness and understanding.

∼

I am a vessel of courage, facing challenges with resilience and determination.

~

I am a beacon of gratitude, appreciating the abundance in my life.

~

I am a source of empowerment, recognizing the strength within me to overcome any obstacle.

~

I am a magnet for love, both giving and receiving it abundantly.

~

I am a guardian of my dreams, pursuing them with passion and dedication.

~

I am a creator of serenity, finding peace within myself and my surroundings.

~

I am a champion for self-reflection, understanding and evolving from within.

~

I am a source of encouragement, uplifting those who may need a supportive word.

≈

I am a magnet for positive connections, attracting relationships that nurture my growth.

≈

I am a vessel of authenticity, expressing my true self with confidence.

≈

I am a beacon of wisdom, learning and growing from every experience.

≈

I am a creator of positive change, contributing to a world filled with kindness.

≈

I am a guardian of my well-being, prioritizing self-care in my daily routine.

≈

I am a source of resilience, bouncing back from setbacks with unwavering strength.

∾

I am a champion for self-love, recognizing my worthiness and embracing my individuality.

∾

I am a magnet for positive transformations, evolving into the best version of myself.

∾

I am a creator of balance, harmonizing the various aspects of my life.

∾

I am a vessel of gratitude, expressing thanks for both challenges and triumphs.

∾

I am a beacon of strength, navigating life's journey with grace and confidence.

∾

I am a source of clarity, making decisions that align with my highest good.

∾

I am a magnet for positive connections, surrounding myself with supportive individuals.

~

I am a creator of purpose, infusing meaning into every aspect of my life.

~

I am a magnet for positive relationships, surrounding myself with those who uplift and support me.

~

I am a guardian of my potential, unlocking new possibilities with each choice I make.

~

I am a champion for gratitude, recognizing the blessings that flow into my life.

~

I am a source of inspiration, inspiring others to tap into their creativity and passions.

~

I am a vessel of resilience, adapting to change with flexibility and strength.

~

I am a beacon of peace, finding tranquility amid life's demands.

~

I am a magnet for success, attracting opportunities that align with my goals.

~

I am a guardian of joy, choosing to find happiness in every situation.

~

I am a creator of positive habits, cultivating routines that contribute to my well-being.

~

I am a source of encouragement, lifting others up with kindness and support.

~

I am a champion for self-acceptance, embracing all aspects of myself with love.

~

I am a vessel of courage, facing challenges with a heart full of bravery.

~

I am a beacon of wisdom, learning and growing from every experience.

~

I am a magnet for positive thoughts, cultivating a mindset that fosters optimism.

~

I am a guardian of my dreams, pursuing them with passion and determination.

~

I am a creator of love, emanating warmth and compassion to those around me.

~

I am a source of empowerment, recognizing the strength within me to overcome any obstacle.

~

I am a champion for self-discovery, continually exploring the depths of my true self.

✑

I am a magnet for abundance, attracting prosperity in both material and spiritual realms.

✑

I am a beacon of kindness, extending compassion to myself and others without judgment.

✑

I am a vessel of balance, harmonizing my life in a way that nurtures my mind, body, and soul.

✑

I am a creator of clarity, seeing opportunities and solutions with a clear and focused mind.

✑

I am a guardian of my well-being, prioritizing self-care as an essential part of my daily routine.

✑

I am a source of authenticity, expressing my true self with confidence and authenticity.

✑

I am a champion for self-love, recognizing my worthiness
and embracing my individuality.

~

I am a magnet for positive energy, attracting good vibes
into my life effortlessly.

~

I am a beacon of resilience, bouncing back from setbacks
with grace and determination.

~

I am a creator of harmonious relationships, fostering
connection and understanding.

~

I am a vessel of empowerment, encouraging myself and
others to embrace their strengths.

~

I am a guardian of my boundaries, ensuring they align
with my well-being and values.

~

I am a champion for self-expression, confidently sharing
my thoughts and ideas.

≈

I am a magnet for meaningful connections, attracting those who uplift and inspire.

≈

I am a source of resilience, facing challenges with grace and determination.

≈

I am a creator of positive impact, making a meaningful difference in the world.

≈

I am a guardian of my thoughts, cultivating a mindset that empowers me.

≈

I am a creator of laughter, finding joy in the simple pleasures of life.

≈

I am a champion for growth, embracing opportunities for personal development.

≈

I am a vessel of self-compassion, treating myself with kindness and understanding.

~

I am a magnet for abundance, attracting prosperity in all areas of my life.

~

I am a beacon of empowerment, inspiring those around me to thrive.

~

I am a source of resilience, overcoming obstacles with unwavering strength.

~

I am a guardian of my energy, choosing to invest it in positive endeavors.

~

I am a magnet for unity, fostering connections and alliances that strengthen the bonds within the black community.

~

I am a guardian of resilience, drawing strength from the stories of black women who stood tall in the face of challenges.

~

I am a creator of positive impact, contributing to a world where black women's contributions are recognized and celebrated.

~

I am a source of encouragement, reminding black women that their dreams are valid, attainable, and deserving of pursuit.

~

I am a creator of positive vibrations, radiating good energy to those around me.

~

I am a beacon of hope, inspiring optimism in myself and others.

~

I am a champion for self-expression, freely sharing my thoughts and feelings.

~

I am a source of encouragement, lifting others up with words of support.

∾

I am a guardian of my aspirations, pursuing my goals with determination.

∾

I am a vessel of love, cultivating deep and meaningful connections.

∾

I am a creator of joy, bringing laughter and happiness into my life.

∾

I am a magnet for positive affirmations, reinforcing my beliefs in my capabilities.

∾

I am a beacon of resilience, facing adversity with a strong and unwavering spirit.

∾

I am a source of kindness, extending compassion to myself and others.

❧

I am a champion for self-improvement, continuously evolving and growing.

❧

I am a guardian of my boundaries, honoring and preserving my well-being.

❧

I am a creator of balance, harmonizing work, rest, and play in my life.

❧

I am a vessel of gratitude, appreciating the beauty in every moment.

❧

I am a magnet for positive thoughts, maintaining an optimistic mindset.

❧

I am a beacon of confidence, embracing my unique qualities with pride.

❧

I am a source of empowerment, recognizing and celebrating my achievements.

≈

I am a champion for authenticity, living in alignment with my true self.

≈

I am a guardian of my time, investing it in activities that bring me joy and fulfillment.

≈

I am a creator of resilience, bouncing back from challenges stronger than ever.

≈

I am a magnet for abundance, attracting prosperity in all areas of my life.

≈

I am a beacon of inspiration, igniting creativity and innovation.

≈

I am a source of encouragement, motivating others to pursue their dreams.

~

I am a vessel of wisdom, gaining insights from every experience.

~

I am a champion for self-compassion, treating myself with gentleness and care.

~

I am a guardian of my dreams, nurturing them with belief and determination.

~

I am a creator of peace, fostering tranquility in my mind and surroundings.

~

I am a magnet for positive energy, attracting good vibes effortlessly.

~

I am a beacon of strength, facing challenges with resilience and courage.

~

I am a source of clarity, making decisions aligned with my values.

~

I am a champion for self-love, embracing myself unconditionally.

~

I am a vessel of joy, finding delight in the journey of life.

~

I am a guardian of my well-being, prioritizing self-care as an essential practice.

~

Love, success, and happiness are rightfully mine.

~

My strength serves as an inspiration to those around me.

~

I embrace and radiate my unique beauty.

~

Success effortlessly flows into my life.

I am the powerful creator of my destiny.

Abundance is my birthright, and I claim it now.

I embody positivity and light.

Confidence is ingrained in my nature.

I am resilient; no challenge can shatter me.

My journey attests to my unwavering strength.

Prosperity manifests in every facet of my life.

Love and joy encompass me daily.

~

Self-love forms the bedrock of my well-being.

~

I am open to receiving life's abundant blessings.

~

Wealth and success effortlessly manifest for me.

~

Each step I take propels me toward greatness.

~

My presence infuses positivity into any space.

~

I exude confidence, self-assurance, and grace.

~

The magic within me is worthy of celebration.

~

Success and abundance are drawn to me.

My mind acts as a magnet for positive thoughts.

I release self-doubt and fully embrace my power.

I emanate love and kindness as a guiding beacon.

I am deserving of life's bountiful offerings.

My happiness is within my control.

I trust in my ability to reach my goals.

I am a masterpiece, a work in progress.

Love, joy, and abundance fill my life.

～

Supportive and uplifting individuals surround me.

～

I am a force for positive transformation in the world.

～

Opportunities leading to success naturally come my way.

～

My heart welcomes both the giving and receiving of love.

～

Resilience and power define me.

～

My potential knows no bounds.

～

Others find inspiration in my journey.

～

I take pride in the person I am evolving into.

~

Confidence and grace radiate from me in every circumstance.

~

Success and prosperity effortlessly flow through me.

~

Positive energy is drawn to my mind like a magnet.

~

I am the architect of my own destiny.

~

Love, success, and happiness are constant companions.

~

Imperfections add to my uniqueness and are embraced.

~

My confidence grows more robust with each passing day.

~

Abundance is drawn to me effortlessly.

~

I am deserving of all the goodness life has to offer.

~

Trusting the journey, even in uncertainty, is my strength.

~

My spirit is unyielding and unbreakable.

~

Positivity gravitates toward me.

~

I attract miracles effortlessly.

~

I release all doubts and authentically embrace myself.

~

Success is my innate state of being.

~

I inspire others to pursue their dreams.

∽

Love and abundance surround me.

∽

Confidence in my abilities to achieve goals is unwavering.

∽

My heart freely gives and receives love.

∽

I am a guiding beacon of light, spreading positivity.

∽

I am deserving of success.

∽

Challenges are opportunities for profound growth.

∽

I am a potent creator shaping my reality.

∽

Positive, like-minded individuals are drawn to me.

~

I am a creator of positive change, contributing to a world filled with compassion.

~

I am a magnet for success, achieving my goals with determination and focus.

~

I am a beacon of authenticity, expressing my true self without reservation.

~

I am a source of empowerment, encouraging others to recognize their strength.

~

I am a champion for resilience, facing challenges with grace and tenacity.

~

I am a vessel of gratitude, expressing thanks for the abundance in my life.

~

I am a champion for self-expression, using my voice to challenge stereotypes and uplift the diverse narratives of black women.

~

I am a vessel of empowerment, advocating for equal opportunities and representation for black women in all spheres.

~

I am a beacon of inspiration, lighting the way
I am a magnet for positive vibrations, attracting joy and abundance into every aspect of my life.

~

I am a guardian of self-expression, encouraging black women to express their creativity without limitations.

~

I am a creator of cultural pride, instilling a deep sense of pride and love for the diverse black heritage.

~

I am a source of encouragement, reminding black women that their voices are powerful and deserve to be heard.

~

I am a champion for self-awareness, embracing the
journey of self-discovery and growth.

∼

I am a vessel of empowerment, uplifting others with
kindness and compassion.

∼

I am a beacon of inspiration, inspiring black women to
lead with confidence and resilience.

∼

# CONCLUSION

As you navigate your daily life, consider integrating these affirmations into your routine. Begin each day by affirming your strengths, acknowledging your worth, and embracing your unique beauty. Carry the positivity of these affirmations with you. Allow them to protect you against doubt and negativity.

Use this book as encouragement during challenging moments. When faced with obstacles, revisit these affirmations to reignite your confidence, and remember the extraordinary legacy of other black women who triumphed over adversity.

Embrace the transformative power of repetition. Incorporate these affirmations into your daily rituals—whether through morning reflections, midday pauses, or evening affirmations. The more consistently you infuse them into your life, the more profound their impact on your mindset, self-love, and overall well-being.

Share these affirmations with fellow black women in your community. Create a culture of empowerment and support. Encourage one another to celebrate individuality, amplify strengths, and overcome challenges. Together, let these affirmations be a catalyst for positive change within your circles.

Remember, this book is a living document—a reflection of your journey as a black woman. Adapt it to your needs and let it serve as a guide that leads you toward success, happiness, and abundance. May these affirmations be a constant reminder of your strength, resilience, and the limitless potential within you. Embrace them, live them, and watch as they help you unfold a life filled with purpose, love, and fulfillment.

# GIVE OTHER BLACK WOMEN THE OPPORTUNITY TO ENJOY THESE POWERFUL AFFIRMATIONS.

We hope these affirmations have been a source of strength, inspiration, and unwavering self-love. Your journey through these pages has been a celebration of the unique essence, brilliance, and resilience that define black women.

Now, we invite you to share your experience. Your voice holds the power to inspire and uplift fellow black women who may be seeking a guiding light. Your review is not just a reflection of your personal journey but a gift to a community that thrives on support and empowerment.

Simply by leaving a review, you are not only supporting a black woman, but bringing awareness to these affirmations and how powerful they can be in our community.

Thank you for your help. You matter, you are important; you are a strong and powerful black woman.

Scan the QR code to leave your review!

www.ingramcontent.com/pod-product-compliance
Lightning Source LLC
Chambersburg PA
CBHW070711130626
46553CB00005B/1938